Learners on the Autism Spectrum

Preparing Highly Qualified Educators

Instructor Manual

Edited by
Kari Dunn Buron and Pamela Wolfberg

AAPC Textbooks
A Division of
APC
Autism Asperger Publishing Co.
P.O. Box 23173
Shawnee Mission, Kansas 66283-0173
www.asperger.net

© 2008 Autism Asperger Publishing Co.
P.O. Box 23173
Shawnee Mission, Kansas 66283-0173
www.asperger.net • 913.897.1004

All rights reserved. No part of the material protected by this copyright notice may be reproduced or used in any form or by any means, electronic or mechanical, including photocopying, recording, or by any information storage and retrieval system, without the prior written permission of the copyright owner.

Publisher's Cataloging-in-Publication

Learners on the autism spectrum : preparing highly qualified educators : instructor manual / edited by Kari Dunn Buron and Pamela Wolfberg. -- 1st ed. -- Shawnee Mission, Kan. : Autism Asperger Pub. Co., 2008.

p. ; cm. + 1 CD-ROM (4 3/4 in.)

ISBN: 978-1-934575-24-6
Accompanied by CD-ROM which contains chapter PowerPoint presentations, chapter tests and a comprehensive exam.
Includes bibliographical references.

1. Autistic children--Education--Study and teaching. 2. Asperger's syndrome--Patients--Education--Study and teaching. 3. Teachers of children with disabilities--Handbooks, manuals, etc. 4. Teaching--Aids and devices. I. Buron, Kari Dunn. II. Wolfberg, Pamela J. III. Title. IV. Learners on the autism spectrum: instructor manual.

LC4717.8 .L435 2008
371.94--dc22   0806

This book is designed in Minion and Adobe Garamond.

Cover Art: Original watercolor by Kari Dunn Buron.

Printed in the United States of America.

Table of Contents

Introduction 1

Overview of Features: Instructor Manual 3

Overview of Features: Textbook 5

Chapter Highlights 7

Preparing for Your Class: Suggested In-Class and Extension Activities 25

Project Ideas 37

References 41

Introduction

As mentioned in the Preface to the textbook version of *Learners on the Autism Spectrum: Preparing Highly Qualified Educators*, we have worked with students on the autism spectrum for over 20 years. We started our careers with very little information specific to autism spectrum disorders (ASD) and often, unfortunately, have had to learn from our mistakes. This shared history drove us to develop university-based programs that address the unique nature of individuals with ASD. We share a common goal – to equip educators and related professionals with the information and tools necessary to plan and implement effective programming for diverse learners on the autism spectrum.

In our research of postsecondary training programs, we found that instructors at the university level were being asked to teach educators about ASD but had few resources that would not only offer a current text for their students, but also provide instructors with practical activities to support their course planning. To fill this gap, we compiled and edited a text written by a diverse group of noted researchers and authors in the field. The objective of the text is to give a comprehensive overview of ASD and to address the reality of the core issues faced by educators today.

This Instructor Manual guides the systematic instruction of current ASD information and offers a myriad activities pertinent to the needs of your students – those who will be teaching and supporting individuals with ASD. We hope it will lay the groundwork for you to create meaningful large- and small-group activities, projects, and enriching discussions. We invite you to use the ideas in this manual and the accompanying CD-ROM that make sense to you and that complement your teaching approach.

An overarching theme of *Learners on the Autism Spectrum* is that successful teaching and learning are rooted in understanding and experience. This volume responds to the critical need to prepare professionals with foundational knowledge and practical skills for educating diverse learners on the autism spectrum. We hope you will find this resource helpful in teaching your students how to translate the theories and research into effective and meaningful practice. Ultimately, this will ensure that individuals on the autism spectrum receive the high-quality education that they deserve.

Overview of Features: Instructor Manual

This Instructor Manual serves as a companion to the textbook, *Learners on the Autism Spectrum: Preparing Highly Qualified Educators,* and includes the following features for instructors' use.

In This Manual

- **Chapter highlights** – Recall the main points of each chapter as a refresher prior to reviewing recommendations for in-class and extension activities, project ideas, paper ideas, PowerPoint™ presentations, chapter tests, and the comprehensive exam.

- **Recommendations for in-class and extension activities** – Refer to the *In-Class Activities* chapter to learn suggestions for in-class and extension activities related to each chapter.

- **Project ideas** – Refer to the *Project Ideas* chapter for ideas that range from those appropriate for assignment at the beginning of the semester, to those to be completed over the course of the semester, to those that are relevant to a particular chapter and should be assigned either prior to or following in-class discussion of a given chapter.

On the Accompanying CD-ROM

- **Chapter PowerPoint™ presentations** – The CD-ROM includes text-based PowerPoint™ presentations that highlight the main points of each chapter. Instructors may add the slide design of their choice to each presentation. PowerPoint™ slides are reproducible for educational purposes in your course only.

- **Chapter tests** – The CD-ROM includes a printable test for each chapter. Instructors may modify these as they wish. They may be shared with students (a) as a self-check of their knowledge and understanding of a chapter's content, (b) as a study guide, or (c) as an in-class test or quiz. Tests are reproducible for educational purposes in your course only.

- **Comprehensive exam** – The CD-ROM also includes a comprehensive exam. The exam largely consists of short-answer questions designed to evaluate the material that constitutes *Learners on the Autism Spectrum*. Instructors may modify the exam as they wish. The exam may be reproduced for educational purposes in your course only.

Overview of Features: Textbook

The *Learners on the Autism Spectrum* textbook contains the following features to help students strengthen their understanding of material discussed in each chapter, as well as share this knowledge with parents and colleagues and apply it to their everyday work with children and adolescents with ASD:

- **Chapter learner objectives** – Refer to the list of learner objectives at the beginning of each chapter for a preview of the chapter's content, as well as to learn what information you are expected to understand and be able to explain after reading the chapter.

- **Vocabulary** – Note the terms included in boldface text within each chapter for at-a-glance reminders of key vocabulary. The definitions of these terms are included in the glossary in Appendix B.

- **Chapter highlights** – Review the main points listed at the end of each chapter to recall the main points discussed within the chapter.

- **Chapter review questions** – Answer the questions at the end of each chapter to check your understanding of and ability to explain the information discussed within the chapter. The review questions may also be used as a study guide when preparing for tests and/or exams.

- **Chapter review answers** – Refer to Appendix A to confirm your answers to the review questions that accompany each chapter.

- **Glossary** – Refer to Appendix B for an alphabetical listing of all vocabulary terms included in boldface text within the textbook (as previously mentioned).

- **Tips for the classroom** – Refer to the final section of each chapter for Tips for the Classroom, designed to provide you with information on how to effectively use the material learned in the chapter while in the classroom or otherwise working with students on the autism spectrum.

Table 1 provides a summary and comparison of the contents of the Instructor Manual and textbook features.

Table 1

Feature	Instructor Manual	Textbook
Chapter Learner Objectives		X
Chapter PowerPoint™ Presentations	X – CD-ROM	
Recommendations for In-Class and Extension Activities	X	
Chapter Highlights	X	X
Tips for the Classroom		X
Chapter Review Questions		X
Chapter Review Answers		X
Chapter Tests	X – CD-ROM	
Glossary		X
References	X	X
Project Ideas	X	
Comprehensive Exam	X – CD-ROM	

Chapter Highlights

Chapter 1

- Autism Spectrum Disorder (ASD) is a lifelong condition.

- Autism Spectrum Disorder (ASD) consists of five subgroups or subtypes that vary in the severity and intensity of the dimensions associated with the disorder.

- The five subgroups are: Autism, Rett's Disorder, Childhood Disintegrative Disorder, Pervasive Developmental Disorder-Not Otherwise Specified (PDD-NOS), and Asperger Syndrome.

- Autism was first described by Leo Kanner in 1943.

- Children with autism are identified as having (a) severe qualitative impairment in reciprocal social interaction, (b) severe impairments in communication, and (c) restricted and repetitive range of interests and activities.

- First signs of autism include sleep disturbance, feeding problems, lack of eye contact and pointing toward objects, preference for consistency, focus on objects rather than people, reluctance to share activities with others, possible fascination with sensory experiences, and failure to imitate others' actions.

- Late-onset autism is when children demonstrate no behaviors of concern until into their second year, after having achieved typical developmental milestones. Reported in 20-40% of cases, children with late-onset autism lose abilities already developed, often over a short period of time, and, by age three, present the same as a child whose onset was early.

- Rett's disorder appears to occur primarily in girls and is a progressive neurological disorder. It is typified by loss of purposeful hand use, hand wringing, spasticity of lower extremities, microcephaly, seizures, and need for supports for daily living.

- Childhood disintegrative disorder, which typically occurs in boys, is a rare condition in which a child develops typically on all milestones until between the ages of 3 and 5. The child then experiences rapid deterioration across all areas to the point that he demonstrates significant and severe difficulties across social, communication, and intellectual skills.

- The category of pervasive developmental disorder-not otherwise specified (PDD-NOS) is somewhat vague but is generally used to refer to children who demonstrate some signs of autism but do not demonstrate a clear diagnosis. The author of the chapter describes PDD-NOS as "fragments of autism."

- Asperger's Disorder/Asperger Syndrome was first identified in 1944 by Viennese pediatrician Hans Asperger, who referred to children with this diagnosis as having autistic personality disorder. In the 1970s, Lorna Wing coined the term Asperger's Disorder to describe children whose profile of autism did not match the diagnostic criteria.

- The current diagnostic criteria for children and adults with Asperger's Disorder/Asperger Syndrome include lack of the significant early language and cognitive skills deficits that are commonly seen in autism, no clinically significant delay in self-help skills or adaptive behavior, and less likelihood of motor mannerisms than seen in classical autism. Asperger's Disorder may not be identified until individuals are school-aged.

- There is some controversy over the diagnostic criteria for Asperger's disorder.

- The term high-functioning autism (HFA) is used to describe children who exhibited classical signs of autism in early childhood but who demonstrated greater intellectual ability (IQ score above 70), social and adaptive skills as they got older, ultimately achieving a level of functioning better than expected.

- While the American Psychiatric Association (APA) discriminates between the classification of HFA and Asperger's Disorder, a number of studies cast doubt on this differentiation.

- The five dimensions/characteristics of ASD are social, communication, cognitive, special interests, and sensory.

- Each dimension can be represented as a continuum, with individuals having more and less significant deficits (being at different stages on the continuum). The level of deficit on the continuum can be indicative of the severity of the disorder in that individual. For example, the child with Asperger's Disorder may have a special interest that is dominant but the complexity and abstractness with regard to that interest represent greater intellectual capacity.

- From the 1940s to the 1970s, autism was thought to be an expression of schizophrenia or psychosis caused by mothers not loving their children/being emotionally unavailable. The term *refrigerator mother* was used to describe these mothers, and autism was seen as a response to this rejection.

- Autism is now considered a neuro-developmental disorder in which specific structures of the brain do not function as expected.

- Research into the causes of autism has investigated: genetics, neurology, possible errors of metabolism, and infections in pregnancy and early childhood.

- Presently, none of the research studies has established a consistent link between immunizations and autism.

- Psychological theories of autism include delayed theory of mind, weak central coherence, and impaired executive function.

- Autism can co-occur with other disorders.

- Children with ASD may develop secondary disorders such as mood and conduct disorders.

- The ratio for autism is 2:1 boys to girls, while it is 5:1 for Asperger's.

- Current estimates of occurrence of ASD range as high as 1 in 150 births.

- There are several possible explanations for why more children are being diagnosed with ASD. These include a broader definition of ASD, realization that ASD may co-occur with other disorders and better diagnostic procedures.

Chapter Highlights

Chapter 2

- Studies of the brains of individuals with autism provide evidence of differences in how their brains are organized and function.

- In the 1960s, it was accepted that autism was of neurologic origin, rather than a psychological or behavioral disorder.

- Once autism was seen as brain-based, the focus shifted to cognition and parts of the brain involved in autism; specifically, the deficit or alteration in the brain and thinking.

- The brain-based and cognitive view of autism led to two different approaches to understanding autism: (a) the core deficit hypothesis/primary deficit and (b) a hypothesis that looks at all simultaneously occurring impairments and intact abilities in an attempt to come up with a common denominator regarding thinking and the brain in autism/ASD.

- The chapter authors discuss several studies of the cognitive basis of autism using individuals with HFA (IQ score over 70). Various intact and impaired abilities were found, demonstrating that individuals with HFA appeared to acquire information on par with neurotypical controls; however, impairments were apparent in more complex processes (see Table 2.1 for specifics).

- The pattern of impairments across domains in individuals with HFA in the studies is indicative of a reduced capability in the area of information processing, with increasing difficulties as the complexity of the task increases.

- In addition to impairments in the social, communication, and reasoning domains typical of the standard diagnostic profile in autism/ASD, the studies also showed impairments in memory and motor domains.

- Tasks requiring multitasking and increased speed of processing put constraints on the information-processing abilities of individuals with autism/ASD.

- Hidden information-processing demands refer to the ability to understand complex sentences or work with tasks that require holding multiple steps in working memory (multitasking).

- Individuals with autism/ASD may store verbal information in chunks and use it in expressive language; sometimes they appear to have greater understanding than they do. Observing actions rather than spoken words may give a better picture of actual abilities.

- The complex information-process concept is of value for intervention purposes by reminding those working with individuals with autism/ASD that it is necessary to convey information clearly and succinctly and recognize that individuals on the spectrum are generally operating in a world governed by facts and rules.

- Complexity as a concept refers to the difficulty of processing information. This difficulty can be caused by certain aspects of the task requirement such as amount of information, structure of information, time constraints on completing task, or multiple simultaneous processing demands.

- Complexity interferes with efficiency in completing tasks for everyone, but the lower capacity for information processing in individuals with autism/ASD means they become limited in this area long before age- and IQ-matched peers.

- *Central coherence* is a term coined in 1989 by Uta Frith to refer to impairments in high-order cognitive and language abilities along with strengths in detail perception and visuospatial abilities in individuals with autism/ASD. Essentially, these individuals have difficulty integrating parts into a whole.

- While the profile of central coherence is similar to the profile found by the chapter authors with regard to information processing, it does not include the sensory, motor, memory impairments, or expressive deficits. Thus, the authors determined that the difficulty for individuals with autism/ASD is better termed information processing so as to address all intact and impaired structures in brain and cognition.

- Functional magnetic resonance imaging (fMRI) allows for recording of brain activity during the performance of cognitive and language tasks. fMRI studies have allowed investigators to observe what occurs in the brains of individuals with autism during different tasks and compare that to what occurs in the brains of neurotypical counterparts.

- fMRI studies have shown that the brains of individuals with autism/ASD have underdeveloped neural pathways (also known as connectivity), less flexibility in changing and meeting different demands, fewer resources to draw on, and less synchrony or harmony in regions working together.

- fMRI studies have also found that individuals with autism/ASD appear to use compensatory strategies, or different cognitive approaches, to completing tasks. These compensatory strategies may assist or interfere with task completion, depending on the strategy and the task.

- Studies have shown impairments in memory and learning exist in individuals with autism/ASD. As in previous studies, the basic abilities appear intact but, as demands and information become increasingly complex, the capacity of individuals with autism/ASD to learn and remember deteriorated.

- Based on studies involving learning and memory, the chapter authors believe the current diagnostic criteria for autism (based on social, communication, and stereotyped patterns of behavior/interests (the diagnostic triad)) needs to be refined.

- While the studies cited in the chapter involved individuals with autism who had IQ scores above 80 and were verbal, the chapter authors believe the findings can be generalized to those with more significant impairments based on the belief that the basis for autism/ASD lies in deficits related to information processing. The progressive reduction in the ability to process information leads to increased severity in functioning, thus creating an intellectual disability.

- This intellectual disability represents what is true for all individuals with autism/ASD: reduced information-processing capacity; a specific cognitive profile. What differentiates low-functioning from high-functioning individuals on the spectrum is level of impairment in connectivity and higher order abilities.

- Implications of the brain basis of autism/ASD involve realizing that individuals with autism/ASD think and perceive the world differently. It is important that interventionists take this into account when working with such students.

Chapter 3

- There is no "typical" child with ASD; there can be dramatic differences in abilities, preferences, needs, and delays.

- There is overwhelming evidence of the effectiveness and importance of early detection and intervention for children with ASD.

- While research indicates ASD can be reliably diagnosed at 2 years of age, the current average age of diagnosis in the United States is 3-6 years of age. For children who are culturally and linguistically different, diagnosis can be even later.

- First Signs, an organization started by parents of children with ASD, has been instrumental in working with the CDC and other medical groups to get the most up-to-date diagnostic information as well as inform the public, through public service announcements and a website, about ASD and early diagnosis. First Signs has also developed a list of developmental red flags that may indicate a child might have an ASD.

Chapter Highlights

- For diagnosis at an early age, most families are referred to a psychologist, developmental pediatrician, psychiatrist, or neurologist for a full evaluation; however, finding professionals who are trained and experienced in diagnosing ASD is difficult in many communities.
- Another avenue for diagnosis is the educational system; however, in many cases children are classified as having a developmental delay rather than ASD.
- It is important to provide families with information on intervention services and community supports after a diagnosis of ASD.
- Parents need to be made aware that ASD is a life-long disorder and that there is no way to predict how an individual child will respond to intervention.
- There are two key issues of debate related to early intervention for children with ASD: (a) the amount of intervention a child should receive and (b) what approach or methodology is most beneficial.
- The authors suggest that, rather than focusing on what program is the "best," the focus should be on what is known about the essential elements of effective programs, including:
  - Sufficient hours and intensity of services
  - Comprehensible environments with access to typical peers
  - Specialized curriculum with an appropriate scope and sequence
  - Family involvement
  - Problem-solving approach to challenging behaviors
  - Appropriate evaluation tools for monitoring progress
- Families need to ask questions before enrolling their children in early intervention programs to ensure the program matches what they see as outcomes for the child, addresses family desires for the child, matches family comfort levels, and has proof of effectiveness.
- Outcome-oriented frameworks of intervention refer to a problem-solving process that is ongoing and based on the child's needs at any given time.
- Meaningful outcomes for children with ASD should improve the child's quality of life.
- Curriculum-based assessment (CBA) is one means of identifying potential skills or outcomes for young children.
- Project DATA, an early intervention program at the University of Washington, is an example of a high-quality early intervention program for children with ASD.
- The core component of Project DATA is an integrated early childhood program with planned and systematic interactions between children with ASD and their typically developing peers. The program emphasizes:
  - Structuring the classroom environment to promote independence, participation, and successful interactions with typically developing peers
  - Developing a consistent schedule and following it
  - Creating the need to communicate with adults and peers
  - Using preferred materials and activities to promote engagement
  - Providing embedded and explicit instruction on valued skills
  - Providing frequent reinforcement and developing effective motivation systems

- Other foundational components of Project DATA are as follows:
  - Extended intensive instruction
  - Technical and social support
  - Collaboration and coordination of services
  - Transition planning and support

Chapter 4

- Social communication involves not only having spoken language but also having an understanding of the function of words and of what others are thinking.
- Theory of mind and communication are intertwined.
- Communication can be defined as the ability to use words to exchange meaning and influence others.
- Individuals with autism may have a rich vocabulary of words but lack an understanding of how to use them to communicate intent or meaning.
- For infants, playing games such as "peek-a-boo" provides opportunities for attention and affect sharing and social reciprocity, which helps the infant develop the interpersonal relatedness needed for later social communication.
- Experiential learning provides infants with the opportunity to develop new neural pathways and increases brain connectivity.
- Infants with autism do not engage in games as do their neurotypical peers and, therefore, miss out on opportunities for emotional regulation, attention sharing, anticipation, and reciprocity with their caregivers.
- Infants with autism tend to engage in repetitive behaviors; therefore, their opportunity to develop connectivity and the possibility that neurons are not "pruned" may lead to less capacity for social-cognitive behaviors, brain function, and concept development.
- Children with autism have deficits in "joint attention;" that is, in the behaviors suggestive of an increasing understanding of the need to engage other minds, such as gaze following, pointing, and showing/offering gestures.
- As brain research supports the relationship between joint attention and theory of mind, including that the two are located in the same region of the brain, children with autism who lack skills in the area of joint attention also have impaired ability to judge what others are thinking.
- Joint attention plays a pivotal role in establishing intentional communication as it is based on a shared awareness (intersubjectivity) and engagement.
- Research shows joint attention impacts typically developing children and those with autism in a similar way in that the amount of joint attention engaged in is highly correlated with vocabulary development and other language and social gains.
- Joint attention sets the stage for intention reading (the ability to "read" another's intent) and is related to the development of symbolic communication.
- Social-pragmatic theory holds that intention reading plays a critical role in language development.
- Social-pragmatic theory can provide a template for what goes wrong in the language acquisition process in autism; specifically, impairments in social cognition in terms of joint attention, affect sharing, and intention reading are seen as likely causes of the pragmatic impairments of individuals with autism.

Chapter Highlights

- While all areas of language may be impaired in individuals with autism (semantics, syntax, pragmatics), deficits in pragmatics constitute the defining language deficit across age and ability levels.

- When a person uses language to express a specific intent, that piece of language is said to serve a particular function.

- In order to use language to serve a function, the individual must possess both pragmatic skills and intention reading.

- Presuppositional knowledge refers to making judgments about the listener such as that of an individual's prior knowledge of the topic in order to decide what information to provide and how to convey it.

- Conversational maxims refer to having an understanding of the rules of discourse.

- Word learning depends on context, knowledge of the underlying concept, the communicative goal of the speaker, word class, and level of novelty.

- Assessment of language for individuals with autism from a social-pragmatic perspective requires certain considerations, including the use of situated pragmatics and naturalistic contexts, evaluating conversational maxims and presuppositional knowledge, and assessing comprehension at both the literal and the discourse level.

- Intervention needs differ due to the variability in functioning levels that exist among individuals with ASD; however, 10 general principles apply across age and functioning levels. The principles include:
  - Intervention must begin where the learner is
  - Intervention should be experiential
  - The use of augmentative means for communication is important
  - Emphasis should be placed on comprehension
  - Active engagement is important
  - Vocabulary targets should be within the individual's conceptual understanding
  - Different classes of words need to be taught differently
  - Intervention should take place in context in order to support the learning of meaning
  - Theory-of-mind activities should be included within language intervention
  - Intervention that promotes generalization of language occurs in contextually relevant routines

Chapter 5

- Structure for students with ASD involves the teacher or caregiver deciding what the learning activities will be, where they will occur, and how long they will last.

- Structured Teaching refers to environmental strategies and environmental supports for individuals with ASD developed by the TEACCH program, a statewide program for individuals with autism in North Carolina.

- Structured Teaching has two main goals: (a) teach the individual with ASD as many skills as possible, given his developmental level; and (b) provide an environment as comprehensible as possible, so the learner can understand the expectations and opportunities around him.

- Structured Teaching is a social-cognitive-behavioral approach applied to the neuropsychological aspects of ASD.

- The "Culture of Autism" refers to the shared neuropsychological patterns of thinking, communication, and behavior commonly seen among individuals with ASD.

- Integral to Structured Teaching is respect for families.

- Five central questions need to be considered and answered for each individual with ASD within Structured Teaching.

- Schedules, task organization, work/activity systems, and routines are integral to Structured Teaching.

  ➢ Schedules are important as they allow individuals with ASD to know where they are supposed to be and what they are to be doing at a given time and allow for predictable environments with knowledge of what will come next. Schedules should be individualized, visual, accurate, and easy to alter should the need arise.

  ➢ Task organization and work/activity systems provide a visual representation of what the student is to do each step of the way during a task or activity.

  ➢ Routines are consistent daily activities for students. A student who has reached independence or mastery on an activity can be considered to have developed a routine (for example, placing completed work in a folder or washing hands before snack time).

- Practical strategies for teachers, including providing visual structure, organizing materials, sharing information, and creating schedules, are integral to Structured Teaching.

- The authors provide multiple examples demonstrating the use of Structured Teaching at different age and ability levels.

Chapter 6

- Sensory processing is a person's way of noticing and responding to sensory events that occur during daily life.

- Sensory systems provide information to the brain, which then forms maps that guide our spatial and temporal orientation, as well as how we react to different situations.

- Sensory processing systems include: touch (somatosensory), body position (proprioceptive), sight (visual), hearing (auditory), smell (olfactory), taste (gustatory), and movement (vestibular).

- Many behaviors observed in children with ASD can be attributed to an imbalance, or poor modulation, of sensory input in the brain.

- Thresholds, or the point at which a particular sensory system responds, can create difficulties: when too low, children may respond too frequently and be distracted; if too high, children may miss important cues.

- In individuals with ASD, arousal input often overpowers discrimination which, in turn, can create unusual behaviors as they try to manage distorted information.

- Sensory systems transmit information to the brain to (a) generate awareness (arousal/alerting) and (b) gather information for brain mapping and discrimination.

Chapter Highlights

- Dunn's conceptual model for understanding patterns of sensory processing combines brain thresholds with self-regulation to create four patterns: low registration, sensitivity, seeking, and avoiding.

- When using a sensory processing framework for intervention, the goal is to improve participation, not change the sensory processing patterns.

- For each of the four sensory processing patterns, the author provides specific information about the pattern, as well as ways educators and others can plan interventions to support student learning based on individual sensory needs.

Chapter 7

- Crisis management refers to a short-term solution to immediately manage potentially dangerous behavior. While crisis management may play a role in terms of dealing with immediate problems, it does not teach the student a prosocial response or appropriate alternate behavior.

- Punishment, which is typically how crisis management is managed (by definition, punishment procedures decrease an undesirable behavior), does not teach appropriate behavior or create an environment of trust and learning.

- Exclusion, another way crisis situations are typically managed, also has limitations in that it may be reinforcing (and thus increase the undesired behavior) if the individual prefers not to be a part of a given activity.

- Perspectives on how to manage behavior have changed from looking at only consequences (reinforcement and punishment) to evaluating the student (including strengths, needs, desires) and the environment (including instruction, classroom management, classroom structure and routines) to design support plans to teach the individual socially valid ways of responding. The set of assumptions on which this change is based include:
  - Behavior is influenced by context
  - Behavior is functional, purposeful, and meaningful
  - Behavior is affected by external events, including emotional and biological conditions
  - Behavior is influenced by factors outside the immediate environment
  - Behaviors will change as people mature and develop new competencies
  - Behavioral supports are guided by a strong value base

- The goal of positive behavior support should be long-term behavior change based on identifying the function or purpose the behavior serves for the individual. This process is called a functional behavioral assessment (FBA).

- Before conducting an FBA, a behavior support team is created to problem solve, support, and guide the process.

- An FBA should lead to intervention to effect behavior change.

- The steps in an FBA and implementation of a behavior support plan are as follows:
  - Defining the behavior of concern
  - Gathering behavioral information
  - Developing hypothesis statements
  - Creating a behavior support plan

- ➤ Implementing intervention
- ➤ Monitoring implementation and outcomes

- When defining a behavior, the first step is to decide whether the behavior in question is a problem or merely an annoyance. Once this has been decided, it is important to describe the behavior in observable and measurable terms so that all involved are clear on what is being measured. Additionally, the behavior must be evaluated in terms of how often it occurs (frequency), how long it occurs (duration), and how strong it is (intensity).

- After the behavior has been defined, data or information about the behavior are gathered. Included in this information gathering is a quest to determine the function or cause of the behavior by examining the relationship between the behavior and conditions in the individual's life.

- Examining antecedents (what happens before the behavior) and consequences (what happens after the behavior) assists in determining what is maintaining the behavior.

- Antecedents fall into two types: *slow triggers* (setting events), which occur before the behavior but not immediately before the behavior, and *fast triggers*, which occur immediately before the behavior.

- Functional behavioral assessments must also take into account variables such as the history of the behavior, strengths of the student, reinforcement history, conditions under which the student does well, type of curriculum used and whether it is a match for the student, amount of structure in the student's day, types of instructional approaches used, occasions when the problem behavior is more likely to be exhibited, the apparent purpose served by the behavior, communication skills of the student, any medical/sleeping/nutritional concerns, and special conditions affecting the student outside the school setting.

- After information on the behavior has been collected, a hypothesis statement is developed about what may be the underlying causes for the behavior. This statement may be based on an underlying behavior pathway, in which setting events, immediate antecedents, behavior, and consequences are outlined about the behavior of concern.

- Behavior support plans using positive support approaches are written based on the hypothesis statements.

- Positive behavior support approaches focus on creating positive learning environments and teaching alternative ways of behaving.

- Curriculum considerations in implementing interventions focus on ensuring the curriculum matches student goals, skills, and needs, and include looking at teaching alternative and pro-social behaviors to replace those that may be problematic.

- Classroom management and instructional considerations focus on ensuring the classroom environment is structured in a positive way that creates opportunities for engagement, includes systematic instruction and clearly articulated expectations, allows for rehearsal, and supports student chances for success. Included are use of routines, consideration of the student's learning style, and teaching strategies for coping with the stresses of daily demands.

- Applied behavior analysis serves as the basis for positive behavior supports. Additionally, specific techniques within applied behavior analysis such as shaping of behavior, creating behavior chains, reinforcing successive approximations, prompting, extinction, and planned ignoring have been used successfully to effect behavior change in individuals with ASD.

- Monitoring and making changes in the plan are essential to ensure its effectiveness.

Chapter 8

- Children with ASD encounter significant challenges learning how to play, socialize, and form friendships with peers due to impairments in reciprocal interactions, communication, and imagination.

- Evidence suggests that children with ASD share the same desires for play, companionship, and peer group acceptance as neurotypical peers.

- Play and social instruction with peers are viewed as a type of intervention that should receive priority in the design and delivery of educational programs for children with ASD.

- Play serves a vital role through which children develop symbolic capabilities, interpersonal skills, and social knowledge.

- Children playing together develop a peer group or "play culture" that is based on active participation in social activities leading to the development of foundational social skills.

- Friendship occupies a central place in children's social lives and serves as a determining factor for social adaptation and adjustment.

- Peer neglect, rejection, or bullying contributes to low aspiration in school performance, depression, withdrawn or isolative behaviors, low self-esteem, and loneliness.

- Many children with ASD demonstrate play that is detached and lacking in imagination.

- Children with ASD tend to stay with only a few activities that they may repeat over and over, with less inclination to engage in functional or pretend play than peers at a similar developmental age.

- While children with ASD vary in their social interaction skills, from seeming "aloof" to "passive" to "active and odd," they all demonstrate fewer interactions, inconsistency in initiating and responding, and difficulties in communication.

- Many children with ASD are excluded from their peer group or "peer culture" because their behavior lacks the culture's definition of "normal."

- Exclusion from the peer group/culture creates a social void caused by peers' lack of understanding of the behavior of children with ASD.

- Carefully planned activities and support are needed to help children with ASD and their peers develop reciprocal interaction skills.

- Friend 2 Friend (F2F) and Integrated Play Groups (IPG) are complementary models designed to support children with ASD in play and friendships with typical peers in inclusive school, home, and community settings.

- F2F is designed to provide a framework for demystifying autism for children aged 3 and up, including puppet programs for 3- to 8 year-olds and simulation games for ages 9 and up; these activities are intended to support typically developing peers in understanding, accepting, and empathizing with children on the spectrum.

- F2F uses a four-step teaching process consisting of modeling, labeling, explaining, and normalizing.

- Within F2F five key learning goals provide the basis for future learning:
  - Recognize and accept differences in self and others
  - Recognize individuals with autism and different kinds of minds as valuable friends

- ➢ Recognize that it is important to ask questions and express feelings
- ➢ Empathize with what it feels like to have autism and different kinds of minds
- ➢ Promote positive relationships with all peers

- F2F introduces seven basic friendship tips involving prosocial communications strategies for peers to use to interact more successfully with children on the autism spectrum.

- F2F includes a puppet program designed to introduce young children to the characteristics associated with ASD. The four-step teaching process is used while never singling out the focus the child with ASD.

- For children aged 9 and above, F2F offers a 50-minute educational presentation in the form of a simulation game designed to help children understand what it feels like to have autism through an exploration of the senses and receptive communication. This is followed by discussion and introduction of the Seven Basic Friendship Tips.

- The Integrated Play Groups (IPG) model is designed to support children with ASD in play experiences with typical peers/siblings as playmates through a system of careful guidance and support.

- Program and environmental design in the IPG model include the group's composition, play space and materials, and play session structure and supports.

- Assessment within the IPG model focuses on systematic observation designed to analyze progress and setting realistic and meaningful goals, including evaluating the symbolic dimensions of play, the social dimensions of play, the communicative functions and means used by the children, and the play preferences and diversity of play exhibited.

- Intervention within the IPG model is based on assessment with guided participation used to implement a carefully tailored and intensive system of supports appropriate to each child's needs and abilities. The adult guides novice and expert players to engage in mutually enjoyed activities that encourage social interaction, communication, pretending, and interactive games.

- Support within the IPG model includes monitoring play initiations; scaffolding play; promoting the use of social communication; and play guidance, in which children are supported in experiences slightly beyond their capacity.

- Play guidance strategies range from orienting to mirroring to parallel play, joint focus, joint actions, role enactment, and role-playing.

- As children become more competent and independent in play skills, the adult lessens the intensity of support provided.

Chapter 9

- "Multiple intelligences" refers to individuals having various types of cognition; social cognition is one of those types.

- Social cognition, self-regulation, and problem-solving skills are important for academic and social achievement.

- Early developmental milestones in social cognition include joint attention, early symbolic communication, imitation of movement, and the simultaneous development of language.

- Students with Asperger Syndrome often develop strong academic cognitive skills but lack social cognitive skills.

- Cognitive behavioral interventions seem to offer social skills learning opportunities for students with ASD who can use metacognitive strategies to explore their own behavior.

Chapter Highlights

- Treatment options vary in terms of how and what to teach with regard to social skills/social cognitive development based on the strengths and needs of the individual on the spectrum.
- If social skills are considered in the context of sharing space effectively, the breadth and variety of skills becomes more apparent, including unwritten rules of behavior for different settings and contexts, adjusting behavior based on circumstances, and understanding what others may be thinking.
- Perspective taking involves understanding that others may have thoughts that are different from yours about your behavior and monitoring your behavior based on those thoughts.
- Many students with ASD lack skills in perspective taking.
- The ILAUGH Model of Social Cognition was developed both from research and from studying individuals with ASD.
- The ILAUGH model serves as an acronym to represent six points to help explain what constitutes social cognitive functioning:
  - (I) initiating communication
  - (L) listening actively with eyes and brain
  - (A) abstract and inferential thinking
  - (U) understanding perspective
  - (G) getting the big picture
  - (H) humor and human relatedness
- Social thinking is not only for the purposes of socializing but is also required in interpreting socially abstract concepts such as problem solving, effective communication, and interpreting curriculum that requires socially abstract thoughts.
- From grade 3 onwards, students are required to demonstrate more socially abstract thinking, both in terms of developing successful social interactions and relationships and in terms of successful academic achievement.
- It is not uncommon for students with Asperger Syndrome to appear to "get worse" as they become older. This reflects their difficulties in navigating an increasingly complex social and academic world.
- Different types and levels of ASD require different social skills interventions due to differences in social cognition, general intelligence, and associated language levels.
- When teaching students with "classical" or "moderate" autism, using metacognitive strategies is not effective. These students require a focus on developing functional communication and academic skills with a clear understanding of behavioral expectation. This should be taught through explicit instruction, consistency, and with the use of clear visual supports.
- Students with HFA are often near-normal or above-normal in academic intelligence and have developed functional communication systems, but have great difficulty in perspective taking, causing problems with understanding implied meaning both from text and from group dynamics.
- Students with Asperger Syndrome can benefit from a metacognitive approach to teaching social thinking and related skills.

- The "four steps of communication" for teaching social thinking are:
- Teach that interpersonal communication is predictable:
  - First, think about the person before speaking to them
  - Second, establish a physical presence
  - Third, use your eyes to think about the person
  - Fourth, use language to relate to the other person
- A variety of programs have been developed to teach students with ASD social thinking and related skills. These include:
  - *Social Stories*™, which provide concrete information about social expectations in specific contexts
  - *Comic Strip Conversations*™, which use character thought and speaking bubbles to help students understand why someone said or did something
  - *Social Behavior Mapping*, which shows students how our behaviors impact the feelings of people around us and how others' perceived thoughts about us impact our behavior
  - *The Incredible 5-Point Scale*, which is used to help students understand their level of anxiety and use strategies to manage it.

Chapter 10

- Individuals with ASD demonstrate difficulties gathering, integrating and interpreting the nonverbal information required to understand the emotional and mental states of others.
- The chapter offers a review of research studies regarding the abilities of individuals with ASD in terms of emotional recognition.
- Studies involving facial recognition of emotion indicate that, while some individuals with ASD who are high functioning are able to recognize basic emotions (happiness, sadness, fear, anger, surprise, and disgust), they still struggle with recognition of more complex emotions.
- Neuroimaging (fMRI) and behavioral studies of facial emotional recognition demonstrate that individuals with ASD process faces differently from neurotypicals, with parts of the brain showing less activation.
- While studied less frequently, emotional recognition from voices also demonstrates less brain activation occurring in individuals with ASD. As with visual recognition, individuals with ASD demonstrate difficulties in vocal recognition of emotion.
- Similar results of reduced brain activation and difficulties with emotional recognition have been shown in studies requiring individuals to use context and those requiring use of multimodalities (such as in real-life situations).
- Individuals with ASD have been shown to be attentive to detail and to prefer a predictable, rule-based environment.
- Given the good skills in systemizing shown by individuals with ASD, the chapter authors hypothesize that high-functioning individuals may be taught a system for understanding emotions/developing better emotional recognition across modalities and complexity.

Chapter Highlights

- In reviewing attempts to teach emotional recognition to individuals with ASD, the authors point out that instruction has focused primarily on social skills development rather than emotional recognition and has taken place in group settings, which make it difficult to individualize pace.

- Computer-based training has also been used to teach emotional recognition with successful outcomes, but generalization of the learning has not occurred. Additionally, the computer-based programs focused on only basic emotions and on facial expressions.

- The benefits of using computers include less potential stress for the individual with ASD, working at one's own pace, the ability to repeat lessons, and the potential for increased interest and motivation.

- The majority of the chapter focuses on the use of a computerized program to teach emotional recognition, *Mind Reading*. This program is an interactive guide to emotions and mental states and was designed to systematically train basic and complex emotional recognition in both visual and auditory channels with life-like faces and voices.

- A study using the *Mind Reading* program over a period of 10-15 weeks with adults with Asperger Syndrome/high-functioning autism (HFA) was described. In the study, individuals used the software independently and were assessed both in terms of their improvement in emotional recognition and in their ability to generalize the newly acquired skills.

- Results from the study indicated the intervention was successful, with significant improvement in the ability to recognize complex emotions and emotional states from both faces and voices. However, generalization remained a problem.

- The chapter authors hypothesize that, by using a program that focused on the strong systemizing skills of individuals with high-functioning ASD, they were able to teach a system that improved emotional recognition but also created a limiting factor in that, by being so focused on the system or rules, individuals with ASD were unable to generalize to situations that lacked the rule-governed nature of the training tasks.

Chapter 11

- Many individuals with ASD leave high school with inadequate social and communication skills for life success, often leading to difficulties in obtaining and sustaining employment as adults.

- IDEA 2004 mandates that transition services be implemented at age 16, or as early as age 14 if deemed necessary.

- Transition services include an individual transition plan (ITP) in which a coordinated set of activities is specified for the individual student. These activities are to be outcome-oriented; based on individual needs; and include instruction, community experiences, and the development of employment and other post-school living objectives.

- Transition teams include the individuals who are part of the IEP team but may also involve members of vocational services, agencies that focus on vocational support, representatives of postsecondary educational options and residential services, as well as others as appropriate.

- Students should be involved in the transition team to the best of their ability. Students should also be made aware of who transition team members are, as well as their rights under the law. Additionally, students need to be taught skills to enhance their participation in their own transition to post-school life.

- ITPs should be individualized and include assessment; the student's preferences; career goals such as academics, career awareness and development, as well as work habits and behaviors; self-advocacy goals such as decision making and self-awareness; and independent living goals, such as taking care of personal needs, community participation, household responsibilities, leisure activities, and managing finances; the steps, instructional methods, and resources to achieve these goals; and methods for evaluating success of transition activities.

- Services and supports for preparing students with ASD for employment and adult life should be based on an assessment of their characteristics and needs. The Underlying Characteristic Checklist (UCC) is an informal assessment tool designed to look at patterns of characteristics specific to individuals with ASD; it can be used to assess and then help in planning intervention based on the results.

- It is important to take into account the student's interests, strengths, skills, tolerance for various stimuli, and supports when creating transition plans.

- Effective planning for and support of the transition process needs to include self-advocacy, self-determination, and person-centered planning.

- Making Action Plans (MAPS) and Planning Alternative Tomorrows with Hope (PATH) are two resources that assist in person-centered planning by looking at hopes for the future as well as the student's current skill level related to those hopes and using that information to develop strategies that will lead to success.

- Strategies for self-determination and self-advocacy must be directly taught to students with ASD. This can be achieved through a variety of means, including scripting dialogue, video modeling, and teaching students about their disability.

- Using the ITP to assist in selecting meaningful coursework based on students' special interests, goals, skills and needs as related to those goals, and requirements for generalization is a critical use of the ITP.

- Students with ASD have documented difficulties in the area of employment, including issues with sustaining employment, social success, job skills, communication with employers and colleagues, and level of income.

- Increasing job placement opportunities for students with ASD should be addressed in secondary school through appropriate experiences; matching the student's interests, skills, and needs with job placement; and matching the type of job to the type of thinking unique to that individual.

- Physical and social aspects of the job need to be considered in matching the individual to a particular job.

- Jobs may be categorized as competitive employment, supported employment, and secured or segregated employment. Most research related to employment of individuals with ASD focuses on the latter two forms of employment.

- It is important to prepare employers to work with individuals with ASD. Such preparation may include strategies for job modification, supervision, coworker relationships, and support services.

- Teaching social behaviors necessary for work and for community involvement should be part of the ITP considerations.

- Students with ASD may consider pursuing postsecondary schooling as an option. If so, the ITP must include information about the student's strengths and needs in terms of self-advocacy and independency.

- Students with disabilities, including ASD, can obtain specialized services and accommodations at the postsecondary level. However, they are responsible for requesting the services and providing documentation of need.

Chapter Highlights

Chapter 12

- It is important that all those working with a student with ASD communicate with one another and share information about what they know of how the student learns, the student's strengths and challenges, and how they meet the student's needs.

- Educational support and intervention teams are mandated by law. They are comprised of teachers, paraprofessionals, administrators, other service providers (such as speech and language therapists, occupational therapists, and behavior specialists), both in and outside of school, family members, and the student him/herself.

- Collaboration among team members can benefit all members of the team. When collaboration is based on a shared focus and shared knowledge of the student's challenges and strengths, the chances for student resiliency and school success are increased.

- Each team member brings different perspectives and knowledge to the collaboration, leading to opportunities for discussion that can result in greater opportunities for student success.

- Collaboration can be either formal or informal.

- The purpose of formal team meetings can be to initiate evaluations for a student not receiving services, to review progress for a student already being served, or to develop goals and objectives/benchmarks.

- Students can receive special educational services either through an individualized education program (IEP) if they meet eligibility requirements as a student with disabilities under federal law or through a 504 Plan if they are able to function adequately in the general education classroom with accommodations.

- Informal collaboration, which can occur at any time, gives all participants on the team the opportunity to address concerns and issues as they happen.

- Areas of importance or concern on behalf of a student may include language and communication, social-emotional issues, behavior, and academics and learning.

- Modifying assignments and providing accommodations can help keep the student from becoming too overwhelmed by school.

- Effective planning and preparation for team meetings may involve any and all of the following: formal assessments; observations of the student; developing goals and benchmarks; examining progress in terms of long-term, adult-outcome goals; future planning to reach long-term goals; and preparing the student to be actively involved in the meeting.

- Factors that contribute to positive and effective communication include (a) openness among team members as well as a desire for mutual understanding; (b) awareness of the student's strengths and challenges and how they impact learning; (c) respect for the student's perspective and a desire to help the student understand the perspectives of others; and (d) a desire to create a manageable environment for the student.

Chapter 13

- In the early 1970s doctors often told parents of children identified with ASD to institutionalize their children and that autism was incurable. At that time, the cause of autism was still seen as based on a reaction of children to cold, non-loving mothers.

- Siblings can be very important to the positive development of individuals with ASD.

- Pre-PL 94-142, options for schooling for individuals with ASD were limited, and the public schools did not have to even accept students with disabilities.

- PL 94-142 was essentially the civil rights law for individuals with disabilities.

- Families and teachers need to serve as advocates for children with ASD.

Chapter 14

- The chapter author describes experiences from pre-K through high school.

- Some of the areas the chapter author stresses as being of particular importance include:

  - Developing a relationship between instructor and learner

  - Engaging students through use of their special interests

  - Teaching the "hidden curriculum"

  - Realizing that individuals with ASD tend to be very literal in their thinking and taking this into account when teaching

  - Making use of assistive technology as appropriate

  - Understanding that many individuals with ASD are victims of bullying. It is important that school personnel are aware of this and take steps to deal with it.

  - Being aware that structure is an important part of a comfortable environment for persons with ASD

  - Understanding that persons with ASD have sensory integration and modulation challenges

  - Involving students in educational planning so self-knowledge and self-advocacy skills are developed

Preparing for Your Class: Suggested In-Class and Extension Activities

Recommendations are grouped by chapter and are listed in order of the textbook material they complement. The heading for each activity is followed in parentheses by the textbook page number with which it corresponds.

Chapter 1

- As a class, discuss the differences and similarities between HFA and Asperger Syndrome with regard to whether the two can be considered separate diagnoses. (pp. 24-25)

- Ask students to come to class prepared with information on something that is a special interest of theirs. In pairs, have students spend 5 minutes telling the other about the interest. For debriefing, have members of the pair indicate the cues (verbal and nonverbal) that led them to change the way they were explaining something, how they knew when to move on with a topic or expand on it, and how they realized the listener didn't understand, was bored, and so on. As a class, discuss the responses from members with regard to theory of mind and how lacking these skills may affect social interactions. (p. 27)

- Provide students with sensory overload, such as extremely bright lights, loud music, and sandpaper to rub on their arms. Continue teaching for 5 minutes during each overload experience. Discuss as a group how these overloads interfered with learning and relate it to students with ASD in the classroom and how they may be affected. You may also wish to try the sensory simulation activities in the kit *Sensory Processing Disorder: Simulations & Solutions for Parents, Teachers and Therapists* by Jenny Clark Brack (2006). (p. 28)

- For 5 minutes, have students reflect in writing on what it might have been like to be told they were the cause of their child's autism because they were "emotionally unavailable" and a "refrigerator mother." Do a Think-Pair-Share activity in which students share with each other in pairs their written reflections, and then briefly discuss as a class the potential impact on parenting this could have had on mothers. Another option is to view the video *Refrigerator Mothers*. (p. 29)

- Bring to class one of the "what is different in these two pictures" activities commonly found in newspapers and magazines. Have students look for the differences between the two pictures, focusing on the small details that have been changed. Then ask the students to turn over the paper (or remove it from the overhead) and ask them to give you the overall theme or gist of the pictures. As a group, analyze how looking at details can distract from understanding the whole. (p. 32)

Chapter 2

- Have students discuss briefly the multitasking that typically takes place in the classroom (e.g., they listen to the instructor and decide what material is important based on vocal intonation, etc.; follow any visuals [PowerPoint™ presentations, overheads]; take notes; keep an ear out for peer discussions, etc.). Set up a 10-minute period when students are unable to multitask: Tell them they are not allowed to write notes, give them each a set of ear plugs, and then continue teaching. After 5-10 minutes, have them remove the earplugs and discuss whether their level of anxiety went up or down and why. (pp. 49-50)

- Give each student a piece of paper and a pencil. Rapidly give a series of simple directions for drawing an object without repeating any of the instructions. Students are not allowed to ask each other what you said. Then, have students turn the paper over and rapidly give another set of directions using more complex grammatical constructions. Debrief with the group, discussing frustration level, information-processing demands, what would have made the task easier, and so on. (pp. 50-51)

- Have students complete a series of motor movements such as skipping while clapping hands over their heads to help illustrate the term *complexity*. As a group, discuss various forms of complexity. (pp. 52-53)

- Use the case examples on pp. 51-52 to discuss the concept of literalness. Have students reflect on any students they may have worked with who demonstrated such behavior and ways in which understanding it might have helped/did help in working with the student.

- Prior to class, review Temple Grandin's book *Thinking in Pictures: And Other Reports from My Life with Autism*. Bring examples of her descriptions to class and share with students. (p. 56)

Chapter 3

- Have students review the three scenarios at the beginning of the chapter. Draw lines on the board to represent continuums of language, cognition, and social skills/behavior, with the left side representing more difficulty, the right side less difficulty in each area, and the middle average difficulty. For each child, have students discuss where he or she might fall on these lines in each area. Use this to demonstrate the concept of a spectrum disorder where different children have more or less difficulty in different areas. (p. 67)

Preparing for Your Class: Suggested In-Class and Extension Activities

- Bring in videos demonstrating the Denver Developmental Profile II, the Assessment, Evaluation and Programming System, and other early assessment tools, as well as copies of the assessment protocols and various developmental checklists. Show clips to students to demonstrate both what might be considered typical development and how the assessment is implemented. Discuss the first signs given on p. 69 of the text and how the assessments and checklists might be used to determine whether a child is in need of intervention or whether they are able to do so. (p. 69)

- Conduct a Think-Pair-Share activity. Have students discuss in pairs how a lack of an educational diagnosis of autism or ASD prior to age 6 or 9 (many states use "developmentally delayed") may affect the type and quality of intervention provided. (pp. 69-70 and pp. 71-73)

- On an overhead or a whiteboard, have students list things that are important to them in terms of their quality of life. Discuss similarities and differences in students' lists and address how these are things to consider when speaking with parents whose child has been identified with ASD, as well as what should be said to families and how one might say it. (pp. 75-76)

- Prior to class, have students visit the Project DATA website (http://depts.washington.edu/dataproj) to review information about the project in conjunction with what they read in the text. Assign different students to view the various presentations offered on the site. Discuss as a group what students learned and the key elements in effective early intervention programs for young children with ASD. (pp. 76-81)

Chapter 4

- Bring to class a collection of common play objects (e.g., a ball, a set of blocks, a doll with moving parts). Split the class into groups of 2 or 3 and have each group generate (in a 5- to 10-minute period) a list of activities that the play object could be used for. Regroup as a class and discuss each item's use in firing brain neurons and concept development, as well as whether some objects might be more useful than others in so doing. Discuss also the effect of limited play schemas on how a child with ASD might approach these same objects. (pp. 92-93)

Possible examples:
- ✓ Ball: roll, bounce, throw (to others, against wall and catch, in air and catch), kick, roll on, spin like a top, sit on, and roll around.
- ✓ Blocks: build a tower or any other building construction, create a boat, use as a car, build a road, and make a pattern.
- ✓ Doll: dress and undress, make arms move as though wants to be picked up, make legs kick as though happy or angry, engage in all care-taking types of activities, such as feeding, bathing, walking in stroller, etc., stand up and make legs move as though walking.

- Show video clips of infants/toddlers engaged in joint attention activities with adults. Discuss as a group behaviors indicative of joint attention (pointing, commenting, showing/offering gestures, gaze following) that they see in the clips. Also discuss the role of the adult in maintaining joint attention and demonstrating for the child intention reading, as well as aspects of intersubjective engagement. YouTube and Videojug offer several examples of each. (pp. 94-96)

NOTE: See *Project Ideas*. Videotaping joint attention is a project idea; you could use those tapes for this activity if that project is used.

- Group students in pairs for this PB&J activity (presuppositional knowledge). Provide each pair of students with two pieces of bread, peanut butter, a knife, spoon, fork, and a plate. Place a divider between the partners. One member gives directions and the other follows. The direction giver tells the follower how to make a PB&J sandwich. The follower MUST follow the directions exactly (i.e., if something is out of order or unclear, the follower follows the directions regardless). At the end of the exercise, see what the sandwiches look like and if they are complete. Regroup and discuss the need for presuppositional knowledge (such as what a knife is), clarity, and sequencing in instructions in order for the task to be completed. (p. 98)

- Provide students with several words that have multiple usages/meanings/functions – perspectival quality of words based on word class. Examples include *run* (to go fast, a tear in pantyhose, a series of wins [run of luck], a car functioning well); *dash* (rush, a small amount of something); *file* (something for shaping nails, a folder for papers, a verb meaning submit something [file a claim]; *bat* (a mammal, an object, a verb meaning to hit something). Various websites provide additional examples (e.g., www.webenglishteacher.com/multmean.html, http://www.manatee.k12.fl.us/sites/elementary/palmasola/ps4mm1.htm).

First have students come up with different usages/meanings, then discuss how the word needs to be in context in order for meaning to be understood. (p. 100)

Chapter 5

- Discuss with the class the concept of answering the five questions for the learner. For example, how do they know the answers to these questions in your class? Are there different answers in other classes they have? How do they know the answers are different? At work, how do they know the answers to these questions? (p. 121)

- Review with students the application examples provided in the text to demonstrate how to implement Structured Teaching. Discuss how answering the five questions for the learner varies based on age and level of functioning (pp. 126-133). After completing the above, have students reread the opening scenario (p. 155) and examine how Structured Teaching was implemented to help Anthony (as described on pp. 133-135).

Chapter 6

- Relate back to the activity in Chapter 1 when students were placed in a situation of sensory overload. Discuss which areas of sensory processing were affected and relate students' responses back to the chapter information. (p. 141)

- Invite an occupational therapist to the class to discuss materials used with individuals who demonstrate sensory integration issues. Ask him/her to bring different materials to allow students to see the materials (such as weighted vests, textured seat pillows, etc.) in order for them to gain a better understanding of the issues and how interventions work. (pp. 142-144)

- Ask class members for examples of students with whom they work who demonstrate sensory processing patterns that are different from peers'. Ask students to determine whether the behaviors fall into the *Seeking, Low Registration, Sensitivity,* or *Avoiding* patterns presented in the chapter. Have students come up with possible interventions based both on the pattern and on the intervention considerations presented in the chapter. (pp. 146-154)

- View the video: *Sensory Challenges and Answers DVD* by Dr. Temple Grandin.
(Publisher's Description: As a child, Temple Grandin could not speak. Her mute, expressionless existence was broken only by rhythmic rocking and occasional fits of screaming and thrashing. In her DVD, Temple draws from her personal and extensive professional expertise on the subject of autism. She focuses on the sensory challenges people with autism experience day to day and coping strategies for dealing with a world full of loud noises, strong smells, chaotic environments, and other sensory assaults.)

After viewing the video, discuss the different sensory systems and how each was an issue for Dr. Grandin, as well as what was helpful to her. Discuss factors to consider when selecting interventions for individual children, pointing out that one approach does not work for all.

NOTE: Several videos are available on sensory integration. Search the Internet for other options if the above video is not available. You may also wish to try the sensory simulation activities in the kit *Sensory Processing Disorder: Simulations & Solutions for Parents, Teachers and Therapists* by Jenny Clark Brack (2006).

Chapter 7

- Give students examples of behavior that is not stated in measurable terms and have them tell you a measurable/observable alternative that might describe such a behavior (this can be done on an overhead/whiteboard as a group). (p. 166)

    Possible examples:
    ✓ Acts impulsively
    ✓ Bothers other people
    ✓ Is distracted

✓ Likes to be silly
✓ Touches everything
✓ Doesn't pay attention
✓ Causes trouble
✓ Is playful
✓ Is irritating

- After explaining the antecedent-behavior-consequence (A-B-C) pathway, provide students with various examples that fit the A-B-C pathway. Then ask them to think of an example of A-B-C in their lives. Allow 5 minutes and then have students share with whole group. (pp. 167-168)

Sample A-B-C examples:

A	B	C
Child sees candy at checkout counter	Child screams and reaches for candy	Mother gives a candy bar
Andrea gets in the car	Andrea lights a cigarette	Andrea thinks she feels less stressed
John is handed a math worksheet	John puts his head down on the desk	John's teacher comes over and offers help

- Provide students with an example of a completed functional behavioral assessment on a student (with personal/identifying information omitted). Discuss how it was conducted, and so on. (pp. 168-171)

- Provide students with various short scenarios and have them work in small groups to put the information into problem behavior pathways. Regroup as a class and discuss how each group placed information in the pathway. (p. 172)

Examples of short scenarios:
✓ Jeffrey didn't want to get out of bed this morning. His mother had to force him to dress and get on the bus for school. Upon arrival in the classroom, Jeffrey threw down his backpack and jacket, ran to the teacher, and started hitting him. The teacher told Jeffrey to stop, asked him what was wrong, and took him to the reflection couch to discuss the behavior.
✓ After attending a funeral for a family member, Sara returned to school. When she saw another child in class crying, Sara began to scream "Who died?" repeatedly. Classmates were initially startled but then began to laugh. The teacher asked the paraeducators to remove Sara from the room.

- Provide the students with examples of behavioral objectives written in the negative and have them rewrite them as a group into positive formats. (p. 173)

Examples of negative to positive:
- ✓ Don't drop book bag on floor → Place book bag in cubby
- ✓ Stop bothering other children → Remain in seat
- ✓ Stop getting upset over what other people say → Develop strategies for responding to others' comments

- Show students the video *Samantha: A Story about Positive Behavioral Support.* (1995). Length: 29 minutes. (This video follows a student with autism, Samantha, as her educational team struggles to address her challenging behaviors. The video illustrates the use of positive behavior support procedures, including functional assessment of problem behaviors, support plan development, and plan implementation. Interviews with family members, peers, paraeducators, educators, building administrators, and others highlight issues involved in this process. For ordering information, call the Experimental Education Unit, Center on Human Development and Disability, University of Washington, at 206-543-4011.)

After viewing the video, discuss as a class how it relates to the information gained from the chapter about FBA and PBS.

NOTE: Even though somewhat dated, this video is an excellent resource to show FBA, PBS, and Circles of Friends.

Chapter 8

- View the video: *Intricate Minds: Understanding Classmates with Asperger Syndrome.* After viewing the video (12 minutes long), discuss (a) what students learned about how persons with ASD think, (b) how this video might be used with secondary school students (it is designed for students grades 7-12) to help them understand how students with ASD process information and why they behave the way they do. (No particular page; serves to set the stage for discussion.)

- View the other two videos in the series, *Intricate Minds: Understanding Classmates with Asperger Syndrome II* and *Intricate Minds: Understanding Classmates with Asperger Syndrome III.* These videos are designed for grades 3-6. Follow the directions for the task as above. (No particular page; serves to set the stage for discussion.)

- Using wireless connection, take students to the following website: http://www.autismnetwork.org/modules/social/circle/index.html and go through the process of Circle of Friends, including how to develop friendship maps, how to use the program, resources, and so on.

Print out the article "Why you need a circle of friends" (http://www.articlesbase.com/health-articles/autism-special-needs-and-the-benefit-of-a-circle-of-friends-pt-2-304464.html) and give to students to read prior to class. Another helpful resource is *With Open Arms: Creating School Communities of Support for Kids with Social Challenges Using Circle of Friends, Extracurricular Activities and Learning Teams* by Mary Schlieder (2007).

Discuss how the practices of the Friend 2 Friend and Integrated Play Groups model complement and extend Circle of Friends. Brainstorm ways in which these practices could be integrated together in the classroom and carried over to other natural settings in the home and community.

NOTE: The kit (consists of DVD, manual and coloring books) *That's What's Different About Me! Helping Children Understand Autism Spectrum Disorders* (2006) illustrates the main points of F2F. The field manual *Peer Play and the Autism Spectrum: The Art of Guiding Children's Socialization and Imagination* (2003) provides IPG tools and techniques and includes a variety of field exercises that may be used for class activities.

- Bring in books designed for children on the topic of friendships and understanding peers with ASD. Some suggestions are listed in the reference section. After separating your class into groups of 3 or 4 students, have them read through the books (all are short) and list ways they could use them in their classes/with younger children to explain the behavioral differences of children with ASD. Regroup as an entire class and ask the students to share what they learned themselves from the books as well as how the books could be used with children. (pp. 185-186)

NOTE: The book *My Best Friend Will* (2005) is a first-hand account by an 11-year-old neurotypical girl about her friend with autism with whom she participated in IPGs.

Chapter 9

- Present to students various scenarios such as going to church or other religious activity, going to a bar, visiting boy/girlfriend or spouse's family, visiting their own families, going to college class. Have them get into groups of 3-4 and discuss the "hidden curriculum" in each setting and how it differs depending on the situation. For example, there are different rules for speaking when they go to church versus a bar. How did they learn them? Do they behave differently with their own family versus in-laws? Discuss issues of sharing space effectively and the hidden curriculum as they relate to these and other situations. (pp. 217-218)

- Using the Four Steps of Perspective Taking, have students consider various situations and discuss as a group their responses (i.e., "Four Steps" of what goes through their minds and how they might modify their behavior/behave). (pp. 218-219)

    Example situations:
    - ✓ Entering this class for the first time and having someone choose the seat beside you
    - ✓ Finding a seat in a crowded emergency room
    - ✓ Sitting in the cafeteria and having someone sit down at a table close to you (even though there are tables farther away)
    - ✓ Working out on the treadmill in the gym and having someone get on the treadmill right beside you

- Give students a scenario, divide them into small groups, and have them (a) write a Social Story™, (b) write a Comic Strip Conversation™, and (c) create a social behavior map to use to explain the situation to the child the scenario focuses on. If you have an Elmo machine, students can create this on regular paper. If you have an overhead projector, give students transparencies and overhead markers. After half an hour, have groups share with the class what they have developed.

Example scenario:
- ✓ John, a 7-year-old with ASD included in a general education classroom, really, really, likes a particular book in the classroom and usually gets it to read when he has time. One day when John goes to get "his" book, another child is sitting on the floor by the bookcase and is reading "John's book"! John stands for a moment and watches, then he goes up to the child and tries to take the book away. When asked by the child, "What are you doing? Leave me alone!" John states, "This is mine," and pulls harder until he gets the book away. Seeing what has happened, the teacher goes over to the boys and tells John to return the book. He refuses; eventually she pulls it away from him, and John starts to cry. The teacher calls the special education teacher and explains what has happened. The special education teacher calms John and writes a (Social Story™) (Comic Strip Conversation™) (social behavior map) to help John navigate and understand what happened. (pp. 225-226)

NOTE: The Gray Center for Social Learning and Understanding provides additional information on developing Social Stories™ at the following website: http://www.thegraycenter.org/store/index.cfm?fuseaction=page.display&page_id=30.

Sample Social Stories™ and other social narratives may be found in the Social Narratives Bank developed by the Kansas Autism Spectrum Disorders Instructional Support Network (http://www.kansasasd.com/KSASD/Social_Narratives_(Social_Stories™_&_Power_Card)_Bank.html).

Chapter 10

- Bring to class several photographs depicting different facial expressions/emotions. For each picture, have students identify the emotion and explain what it was about the face that led them to their conclusion. Discuss common indications such as eyes crinkled at corners, line between eyes, how the mouth, head, shoulders are positioned, and so forth, that might assist in recognizing and teaching facial emotional recognition. (pp. 235-236)

- Invite someone such as a speech/language therapist to the class and discuss body language and how he/she teaches individuals to recognize cues. (p. 235)

- Divide students into age groups (i.e., preschool, elementary, middle/high) and have them identify software programs and other materials that teach emotion recognition. Students can write brief descriptions of the materials, including publication information, cost, time required, how it can be integrated into the curriculum, etc.

- Have students discuss current strategies used in teaching emotional regulation and social thinking. Have them sort out which ones employ the learning strength of systemizing.

Chapter 11

- Provide students with copies of the following prior to class. Use to discuss issues of transition for individuals with ASD, transition planning, questions for speakers (see below) and for personal reference.
    - ✓ *Issues in transition for students with autism.*
      www.projectforum.org/docs/autism_secondary_transition.pdf

    - ✓ *From the Autism Society of America.*
      www.autism-society.org/site/PageServer?pagename=livinghighschool
      NOTE: You may need to register in order to access downloads from the ASA site. Registration is free.

  Ask a transition coordinator from a local school district to come in and discuss the processes involved in his/her program in transition planning. (p. 257)

- Provide students with two different transition plans (with identifying information crossed out or plans created by the instructor specifically for this activity). One plan should be well done and the other poorly done to provide students with positive and negative examples. Divide students into small groups to review the plans in terms of the information supplied in this chapter. Specifically, students are to evaluate each plan in terms of:
    - ✓ Does it appear to be person-centered?
    - ✓ Is it outcome-oriented?
    - ✓ Is it broad-based?
    - ✓ Was the student involved in the planning?
    - ✓ Were all areas of post-school environments addressed?
    - ✓ Did family members state their desires for the student?
    - ✓ See also Table 11.2 on p. 262 for other areas in terms of goals.

  Regroup after about 30 minutes and discuss group responses to each of the plans. Have students suggest ways in which the poorly developed plan could be improved. (pp. 261-262)

- Review with the group the Underlying Characteristics Checklist (UCC) (the social section is shown on p. 264) and discuss how it can be used in developing an ITP. (See Aspy & Grossman in References for obtaining a copy.) (pp. 263-264)

- Ask the person in charge of disabilities services at your college or university to come to your class to discuss the process by which individuals with ASD are evaluated for services, what services are available, the requirements for self-advocacy in term of speaking to professors, and so on. (p. 272)

- Prior to the chapter discussion, refer students to the following site: http://www.autism.com/individuals/learningselfadvocacy.htm from the Autism Research Institute for information on teaching self-advocacy to students with ASD. (p. 265)

Chapter 12

- Take students to the following website, which shows various activities that improve home-school connectedness. Review some of the activities and discuss how they might help students feel more connected to school. http://www.actforyouth.net/default.asp?ID=schoolConnectedness3 (p. 281)
  NOTE: If you do not have access to the web in class, go to site and print out activities of interest to use with class.

- Go to the following website (from Ideas That Work) and read a publication developed by the military. Other than the introduction, the article gives an excellent overview of school connectedness. Print the article and share with students, or refer students to the site and have them read the article prior to class and come prepared for discussion. http://cecp.air.org/download/ MCMonographFINAL.pdf (p. 281)

- Have students discuss the importance of collaboration and how effective teams can improve outcomes for students with ASD. List student responses on overhead or whiteboard. (pp. 282-285)

- The chapter offers many excellent scenarios involving students with ASD from p. 288 onward. Assign different students to cover different scenarios and evaluate the students based on concepts introduced throughout the text.

Chapter 13

- Ask members of a parent advocacy group (specifically for ASD, if possible) to speak to the class about their experiences with pediatricians/first notification, early experiences, effects of ASD on family/siblings, school experiences, post-school employment and living, and so on. If possible, invite parents with children across age groups and ability levels. Prior to the presentation, have students come up with 10 questions to ask to help them better understand how to work with families.

- Using *Autism Advocate* published by the Autism Society of America, select various articles from the Personal Perspectives department written by family members of individuals with ASD. Prior to reviewing the chapter, hand out copies of the personal perspectives, with different groups of students receiving different articles. Ask students to prepare to discuss in small groups the article the group received, and then gather as a whole class to discuss impressions gained from each perspective.

Chapter 14

- Show the video/DVD: *Growing up with Autism*. After viewing the video, divide students into Think-Pair-Share teams and have them discuss what they learned from the video, how the video reflected the stages of autism, the skills, talents and dreams of Taylor Crowe, the family role, and so forth. Regroup and have students share their thoughts. Then hold a class discussion.

- Using *Autism Advocate* published by the Autism Society of America, select various articles from the Personal Perspectives department written by individuals with ASD. Prior to reviewing the chapter, hand out copies of the personal perspectives, with different groups of students receiving different articles. Ask students to prepare to discuss in small groups the article the group received, and then gather as a whole class to discuss impressions gained from each perspective.

- Ask an individual or group of individuals with ASD to speak to your class about their school experiences – what worked/what didn't work, what they think would have been helpful, and so on. Prior to the presentation, have students prepare 10 questions to ask that focus on what strategies helped, special issues (socially and academically), and so on.

Project Ideas

Short-Term Projects

- Have students find and read a book for children on autism. Assign a short paper summarizing the book and how it can be used with children to understand autism and develop friendships/understanding of peers with autism. Have students write also a brief annotated bibliography and send it via email attachment to the instructor. Compile for the group (or have a volunteer compile) a bibliography of children's books on the subject.

- Have students contact local and state early intervention services and find out what services and supports are available for children with autism. Have them create, as if to give to a parent, a resource booklet with information on programs, extracurricular activities, camps, advocacy groups, and so on, locally and statewide.

- Require students to visit 10 websites on autism/ASD and write down information about the site's URL address, the visual look of the site (is it attractive, crowded, etc.), ease of navigation, usefulness and accuracy of the information presented, whether they would visit the site again and why/why not, any references to back up claims made, resources/links offered, and so on.

- Have students contact families with infants/toddlers and request the opportunity to videotape (preferably) or observe them during play, bathing, eating, or any other occasion when joint attention might occur. Have students record the various times when joint attention and intersubjective engagement occurred, what prompted it, how it was demonstrated, how the child or adult maintained it, how focus shifted to something else, whether child/adult followed the shift, and so on. Have students write up their findings and share with class.
  NOTE: A video (with parental permission) is preferable as the processes can be seen.

- Have students view the movies *Rain Man, Cinemania,* and/or *Napoleon Dynamite*. While viewing these DVDs, ask students to write down instances of difficulties in communication, social interaction skills (for example, in *Rain Man*, the title character scares the waitress when she realizes that he knows her telephone number), and other areas specific to social-cognitive understanding. Ask students to provide you with the list of social-cognitive difficulties they observed in the movies and a summary statement of whether viewing the movies helped them better understand social-cognitive issues in ASD and how.
  NOTE: This could also be an in-class activity if clips of the movies were shown to illustrate social-cognitive concepts.

- Have students go to a location of their choice (a shopping mall or other large group setting works well). Tell them that they are to select a location and collect data on a particular person's behavior. As this is an introduction, have them use event recording, or tallying each time the behavior occurs. Have them collect data for 30 minutes on a sheet you supply. Have students write up a brief summary of the experience. When you get to Chapter 7, have students submit the information and share with the class.
  NOTE: Suggestions for data collection (to give students an idea):
  ✓ Count how often a store employee says "Have a good day"
  ✓ Count how often an employee wipes a counter
  ✓ Count how often a classmate tosses his/her hair
  ✓ Count how often the instructor says "um"
  ✓ Count how often a classmate talks to the person next to him/her
  ✓ Count how often the TV newscaster in the morning gives the time

- Interview a transition coordinator/planner from a local school district. Ask about assessment tools used, how contacts with outside agencies are made, interactions with families for planning, any cultural differences that might exist in terms of desired outcomes, who writes the goals, and so on. Have students give you their questions for review prior to the interview. After conducting the interview, students submit the questions and answers, as well as what they learned from the interview process and how it could be used by them in the future.

- Have students interview a parent of a child with ASD and write a report, including the questions and responses, followed by a summary of what they learned and what they will use as teachers/in working with children/individuals with ASD. Questions to be asked should be submitted and approved by the instructor prior to the interview.

Long-Term Projects

- Have students visit a variety of programs in which individuals with ASD participate. They should include early intervention, school-aged, secondary, and postsecondary learning, living, and employment. Students are to describe each environment and relate how what they observed ties into information from various text chapters.

- Have students select a book (a) written by an adult with ASD (e.g., *Beyond the Wall* by Shore, *Born on the Wrong Planet* by Hammerschmidt), or (b) a realistic book about ASD (e.g., *The Curious Incident of the Dog in the Night-time* by Haddon, *The Speed of Dark* by Moon, *My Strange and Terrible Malady* by Bristow) and write a book review to be shared with classmates. The review should include a summary of the book, what the student learned professionally and personally from reading it, and a recommendation as to its usefulness for classmates to read/use in teaching about ASD. The review should be about three pages long (or whatever length you think is appropriate). Students also briefly present the information to the class and hand out copies of their reviews after you have graded them and they have been revised as necessary.

- Have students who are currently in the classroom and working with a child with ASD conduct a functional behavioral assessment on a child for whom one has not previously been done. Using the questions in the chapter on pp. 168-171, the students should collect the information, answer the questions, form hypotheses, and design a possible intervention plan. In the report for the project, the students will provide all of the information noted above, as well as a detailed description of the child (age, grade level, communication skills, etc.).

- Have students who are currently in the classroom and working with a child with ASD design and implement a Circle of Friends project in their classroom and in conjunction with the target student's family. Your students are to go through the steps of designing the program, implementing it, and writing about the results to the point in time in which they hand in information.
  NOTE: For a short-term project, do the above, but only the design part.

- Have students select a textbook chapter that is of interest to them. From that chapter, ask them to select a single topical area. Students then conduct research specific to the topic, using sources such as books, chapters, articles, and the Internet, and write a 10- to 15-page research paper. Students may also be asked to create a PowerPoint™ presentation to submit to the instructor and possibly present to the class.

References

Aspy, R., & Grossman, B. (2007). *The ziggurat model: A framework for designing comprehensive interventions for individuals with high-functioning autism and Asperger Syndrome.* Shawnee Mission, KS: Autism Asperger Publishing Company.

Autism Society of America. (n.d.). *Autism advocate.* Bethesda, MD: Author.

Brack, J. C. (2006). *Sensory processing disorder: Simulations & solutions for parents, teachers and therapists* [Kit with DVD]. Shawnee Mission, KS: Autism Asperger Publishing Company.

Bricker, D. (2002). *Assessment, evaluation, and programming system for infants and young children: AEPS measurement from birth to six years.* Baltimore: Paul H. Brookes.

Bristow, C. (2008). *My strange and terrible malady.* Shawnee Mission, KS: Autism Asperger Publishing Company.

Christlieb, A. (Director) & Kijak, S. (Director). (2003). *Cinemania* [Documentary]. Available from http://www.imdb.com/title/tt0281724/

Crowe, T. (2003). *Growing up with autism* [Video]. Arlington, VA: Council for Exceptional Children.

Experimental Education Unit, Center on Human Development and Disability. University of Washington. (1995). *Samantha: A story about positive behavioral support.* Seattle: Author.

Grandin, T. (1995). *Thinking in pictures: And other reports from my life with autism.* New York: Vintage Books.

Grandin, T. (n.d.). *Sensory challenges and answers DVD.* Las Vegas, NV: Sensory Resources.

Haddon, M. (2003). *The curious incident of the dog in the night-time.* New York: Doubleday.

Hammerschmidt, E. (2008). *Born on the wrong planet.* Shawnee Mission, KS: Autism Asperger Publishing Company.

Intricate minds: Understanding classmates with Asperger Syndrome I, II, III. Available from Coulter Video: www.coultervideo.com

Keating-Velasco, J. (2007). *A is for autism, F is for friend.* Shawnee Mission, KS: Autism Asperger Publishing Company.

Moon, E. (2005). *The speed of dark.* New York: The Random House Publishing Group (Del Rey).

Quinn G. (Producer), & Simpson, D. E. (Director). (2002). *Refrigerator mothers* [Motion picture]. Available from Fanlight Productions 4196 Washington Street, Suite 2 Boston, MA 02131.

Schlieder, M. (2007). *With open arms: Creating school communities of support for kids with social challenges using circle of friends, extracurricular activities and learning teams.* Shawnee Mission, KS: Autism Asperger Publishing Company.

Wolfberg, P. J. (2003) *Peer play and the autism spectrum: The art of guiding children's socialization and imagination* (Integrated Play Groups Field Manual). Shawnee Mission, KS: Autism Asperger Publishing Company.

Books to Use for Suggested In-Class Activity in Chapter 8

Espin, R. (2002). *Amazingly ... Alphie! Understanding and accepting different ways of being.* Shawnee Mission, KS: Autism Asperger Publishing Company.

Gagnon, E., & Myles, B. S. (1999). *This is Asperger Syndrome.* Shawnee Mission, KS: Autism Asperger Publishing Company.

Keating-Velasco, J. (2007). *A is for autism, F is for friend.* Shawnee Mission, KS: Autism Asperger Publishing Company.

Larson, M. (2006). *I am utterly unique: Celebrating the strengths of children with Asperger Syndrome and high functioning autism.* Shawnee Mission, KS: Autism Asperger Publishing Company.

Larson, M. (2007). *The kaleidoscope kid: Focusing on the strengths of children with Asperger Syndrome and high-functioning autism.* Shawnee Mission, KS: Autism Asperger Publishing Company.

Lears, L. (1998). *Ian's walk: A story about autism.* Morton Grove, IL: Albert Whitman & Co.

Lowell, J., & Tuchel, T. (2005). *My best friend Will.* Shawnee Mission, KS: Autism Asperger Publishing Company.

McCracken, H. (2006). *That's what's different about me! Helping children understand autism spectrum disorders* [DVD, manual and coloring books]. Shawnee Mission, KS: Autism Asperger Publishing Company.

References

Peralta, S. (2002). *All about my brother.* Shawnee Mission, KS: Autism Asperger Publishing Company.

Sabin, E. (2006). *The autism acceptance book: Being a friend to someone with autism.* New York: Watering Can Press.

Shally, C., & Harrington, D. (2007). *Since we're friends: An autism picture book.* Centertown, AR: Awaken Specialty Press.

Veenendall, J. (2008). *Arnie and his school tools: Simple sensory solutions that build success.* Shawnee Mission, KS: Autism Asperger Publishing Company.

AAPC Textbooks
A Division of

A PC

Autism Asperger Publishing Co.
P.O. Box 23173
Shawnee Mission, Kansas 66283-0173
www.asperger.net • 913-897-1004